Fatou

My Early Life

Fatima Barry

ISBN: 978-1-938403-04-0

CONTENTS

ACKNOWLEDGMENTS

This work is dedicated to the wonderful, thoughtful and helping individuals belonging to the Guinea Association Community of Austin, Texas.

When needs arise, be it in ill health; financial distresses; deaths in families; or the happy occasions such as marriages, having babies; individuals obtaining outstanding achievements the group is standing by to be of service.

They are willing and able. I am blessed to have such a community group whose door is always open for anyone to join. Thank you all for what you are doing in making this world a finer place.

And also I'm indebted for the wonderful technical assistance from a most talented individual, Antonio Flores. Thank you Antonio!

PROLOGUE

My small country is Guinea in West Africa and I was almost born there, (more on that a bit later). The land is crescent shaped, about the size of the state of Michigan in America. The name of Guinea's exact origin is unknown and thought to be a translation from the Berber language meaning 'burnt people,' and in the long past, most of Africa went by that name. There are four countries with Guinea in their names: Republic of Guinea; Guinea-Bissau; Equatorial Guinea; and an unrelated, derived name of an independent state - Papua New Guinea.

There are six countries encircling my home (starting from the north-west and going clockwise): Guinea-Bissau, Senegal, Mali, Ivory coast, Sierra Leone, and Liberia. The land has four geographical regions: Coastal; Highlands; Central Mountains; and Forested Jungle. The capital and largest city is Conakry on the mid coast.

The population is about 12 to 13 million with French as the main spoken language, although there are more than two dozen indigenous tongues, It is a secular state with around 85% Muslins (mainly Sunni). The political history is a little chaotic after the fall of the last of the African Empires and their replacement by colonization in 1890 as French

West Africa. The following independent, republican governments have had their problems, though slow improvements have been made; but this work is a retelling about me and so we will move on with my own story

Chapter 1: How It All Started

My name is Fatima Barry, I was born on the second day of May in 1987, in a taxi on the road between Senegal and Guinea. It was in a large, but not new vehicle with several other passengers present. My mother, Dalanda had developed strong stomach pains (because of me) and suddenly I had my birth in the backseat!

The nice taxi cab driver had a blanket in the car and one of the passengers was carrying a basket, which was just the right size for me, and because Senegal was closer than Guinea we went to a village named Tamba. That was where an uncle of mine lived and he took us in. Counting me there were now three siblings in my family.

It was one week later that the baby naming ceremony, called Batem, gave me my name: Fatima Barry. The six year old son of my uncle then announced,

"When this baby grows up I will marry her (he was wrong about this)!"

*   *   *

By the next week my mother and I were back home in Guinea and greeted by my excited father. Within two years, my mother was to conceive again, (adding to my two siblings; who were now: my ten year old brother Yaya, and sister Isha, who was eight years old). This newborn was a baby girl, named Lamararm. Unfortunately, my mother died during this child's birth and one week later this baby girl also passed away.

Chapter 2: The Negotiations

My father, Ebrahim, now had three children to care for but luckily he owned a plantation which grew avocados, potatoes, sweet potatoes, mangos, and bananas. In addition he was a successful hunter who supplied meat for our family. After the death of my mother a second wife was needed for the family and father chose a village girl named Saratou. So she was my first stepmother. I was four years old.

We would walk the half hour distance to the market where we would sell our harvest. (The chore of raising three children, and having a new, not so pleasant wife and working the plantation would, later in the future, make him decide to look for an additional wife).

Ebrahim's marriage to Saratou came about in this way: in a village close by, an acquaintance of his had three daughters, all of marrying age, and he made a request to visit them. He was invited for a 'one day' period. My father explained his own problem of needing a wife and was allowed to look the daughters over.

Father made his choice, selecting the middle one, who was said to be a hard worker and two months later, as is the usual time frame in Guinea, Ebrahim sent a request to his close relations to ask for this possible marriage.

While the father of this second daughter, Saratou, fully agreed to this connubial arrangement, (as my stepmother number one), he did so over his own families' advice against it. So one month later she still came to the home of Ebrahim. In time a second stepmother was brought into the family, Fatou. Our family's closeness with Fatou quickly developed but such was not the case with stepmother, Saratou. After this, the three of us and Saratu stayed with daddy and sometimes we children stayed with Fatou at her place. Daddy ran the plantation well and we took our efforts to the market weekly.

*   *   *

A family who desired to have help at their house was told about my father's two daughters who would be available to come and live with them. Father said yes for my sister Isha, but not for me and they came to pick her up and took her to their house in the Capital, Conakry. Father, brother Yaya, and myself stayed on at the plantation. Since both grandmas were blind I did my best to help them when I could.

The grandma, on my mother's side, lived a two hour walk away. Therefore I alternated weeks of being with each of them.

*   *   *

My sister stayed with the family in the capital for one year. She got along poorly with the whole family: the father, wife, three brothers and single sister. She insisted she wanted to come back to our father. Hence, they brought her back but left her down at the marketplace. We were working on the high ground of our elevated farm and daddy looked in the distance along the road toward the market place and said,

"Look, someone is coming up the path with a suitcase on her head. I Think that's your sister coming!"

It was indeed her and we all hugged and kissed as we were so pleased to have Isha back. She said,

"I couldn't stay away from you guys any longer!"

*   *   *

Unfortunately, the older stepmother (stepmother number one) daddy had married two years before, had found she couldn't get along with my brother and sister nor could we with her. In addition, the family in the capital now approached daddy and again requested I come with them and let them raise me. Because my father loved me so much he refused ... and I didn't want to go either.

Chapter 3: Taking Grandma Home

It was one year later my father decided to make a trip to Senegal to visit with his brother in Tamba. His hope was also to obtain products of dry powdered milk and coffee to sell when he returned home. Before this trip my stepmother had delivered a baby girl, named Khadija (after another of Mohammad's wives). Yet my father still allowed me to sleep on his chest every night! And that led to my stepmom's (Saratou) jealousy.

Before daddy had left on his one month visit he had instructed Saratou to take our bananas and potatoes to market to sell, and because I loved meat and bread, to buy some for me. We did sell our produce at the market though she never brought any meat home. But my brother and sister and I ' stayed cool about it' until my daddy returned at the end of the month.

Saratou also demanded none of us would mention a word to him about our strained relationship with her. And as time passed daddy did not like this new living arrangement and finally decided to marry a second wife. Such undertakings are quite commonly done in Guinea society.

*   *   *

It had been within the year and a half daddy chose the second wife, Fatou (stepmother 2). Daddy however, also kept the first wife, choosing not to divorce Saratou as family pressures discouraged him from doing so, (thus showing it was often easier to marry in our country than divorce).

Fatou was very friendly and nice to everyone. She took me often to her house for three day stays or so.

$$* \qquad * \qquad *$$

One day, Oumou, the grandma on my mother's side, came for a visit and at the end of the time invited me to return to her house for a longer visit with her. Daddy suggested I should go, although it was a two hour walk; in mountainous terrain; I was only six; and Oumou was blind! In addition, the only time I had gone there was with my brother who carried me on his shoulders. I knew exactly what this walk would be like.

We set off, I in the lead, holding a rope tied to grandma. At four o'clock with the setting of the sun we left. So we walked, walked, walked, until suddenly the road ended at a deep precipice blocking our way! I started crying as now it was getting dark and the surrounding forest was dense. I turned to grandma and said,

"Let's go back"

She replied, "No, we've come too far."

I insisted, "We must go back, now."

We turned around and walked, walked, and walked as it became totally dark we found we were lost! Not only that, but the sound of the forest animals made us both frightened.

Finally I saw a guy coming toward us, who I thought at first was a fairly large animal. Then I yelled at Oumou, because she was also hard of hearing,

"Something is coming."

The stranger called back,

"Don"t be afraid, it's me, it's me, it's me," and fully approaching said, "what are you guys doing here?"

"We are lost," I said.

But grandma did understand exactly what was happening. It turns out that she knew this fellow.

He said, "You two are completely lost, you don't know the way. Let's go, I will take you home."

As we passed his place along the way back he took us in and fed us. Since then I don't really like it when it is dark outside.

Chapter 4: My Father Goes to Senegal

When I came home and told daddy what happened he was scared,

"Oh my God, what have I done?"

I said, "I will not go alone with grandma anymore!"

"Next time," he said, "your brother and sister will go with you."

*   *   *

This family from the capital now came and asked for me to come and live with them but my daddy responded,

"This little one cares for both grandmas and Fatima gets along very well with them." But this family persisted and even begged, and father did consider permitting this and I said,

"I don't want to go."

He then paused and responded,

"I will think about it."

Finally he realized I missed my mother so much and I continued to cry and cry over her and was so sad at her death and also that he would be gone to Senegal often to purchase the powdered milk and other produce to bring back and sell in our village; he felt is was probably better for this little girl to be raised by a 'full family.' so he said,

"Fatima, I want to talk to you."

"Okay, daddy."

"Do you know the family where your sister went to stay in the capital?"

"Yes, I know."

"I think it is best I send you to them."

"No daddy, no, I don't want to go."

He responded, "I will be traveling often to Senegal and when that is settled, I will bring you back home. I promise!"

"Please don't leave me there, I will miss you so much."

"Okay Fatima."

*   *   *

Thus the decision was made. He set the date for his departure to Senegal within two month's time.

I didn't sleep the four nights before he was finally to leave. I greatly wanted to say goodbye to him the morning he was to depart. He assured me that would be so, saying,

"Baby go to sleep now; I promise I won't leave before saying goodbye."

I had a plan to assure this would be. As is the custom in African houses, there is a central fireplace where a fire is continually kept burning and is well stocked with numerous wooden logs. I did not sleep at all, but got up throughout that night and after removing all but one log (to allow it to give a slow burn) I would add an additional one when it was needed. This way, I thought, it would allow my father to sleep longer in the morning, late enough so that I and the family would be awake to bid him goodbye. The whole family was able to partake of breakfast together. I remember it was a Monday.

*　　*　　*

The plan was for daddy to walk to the market with a friend. He was to meet him at the road after a ten minute walk down to the base of our farm. Thus we all took our breakfast meals down to that point, but the friend never showed up and all the goodbyes were performed at that spot. The road dropped away from the inclined plane of our farm and I stood up on this elevation until I could no longer see the white traditional hat he was wearing, the last time I saw my father.

*　　*　　*

After one month the family from the capital city came for me; and so I left home for good. When I got there I was sad. They said,

"Don't cry, Fatima, your daddy will come to see you - but he never did!"

*   *   *

The first two lonely months drug on and then this Capital Family brought another girl into the group. She was one year younger than me, but more fortunate, as her birth family did not live far away. Yet she cried a lot too.

During this time I was taught to clean the house, sweep the outside porch, learn how to cook, and a number of other chores.

*   *   *

After two years I asked,

"When is my daddy going to come," and they responded,

"Next month he will be here."

And so I counted the days off - he did not come!

I did love the bread and milk I could get and I told myself to be calm and enjoy what I had at least and in that way I would patiently wait for daddy.

*   *   *

Five or six years passed and I finally realized my father would probably never come to me. I was not told he had fallen sick. Within three weeks of his sickness he died!

Before daddy died he wrote a letter and had three copies made: one to my aunt (Asti); one to my stepmother (Saratou); and the last one to my uncle (Muhammad). In the letter my father wrote: 'If I die, send this information to the "Capital Family" that is raising my Fatima. I do not want her to be sent back to Kiri. But in the event you do not want to keep her then you can send her back to the village.'

It turned out daddy got an infected tooth and the disease spread throughout his body. It was his expectation that if he died this family I was living with would be given a copy of this letter.

I had dreamed something bad had happened before his death. That was on a Monday, I think, and by that Thursday, daddy had died. The letter was carried and delivered to us by a bus passenger.

I was playing outside with some friends and one of them saw my 'new' mother crying and came running to me, and informed me of it; I checked it out. As I came toward her she stopped crying and had decided I would not be told until that evening after dinner. First we ate, then I was asked did you eat all your dinner and I said I did. Then strangely they inquired if I was full and again I answered the same way. These questions seemed strange to me and I wondered what was going on. Then my 'new' papa informed me he got a letter from daddy.

I asked, "Is it about my father; is he coming?"

The papa said, "No."

I asked, "What has happened?"

He responded, "Your daddy got sick."

"Is he okay; can he come here?"

Papa (Saedou) answered, "No, I'm sorry ... he is dead!"

Stunned, I replied, "Okay, no mom, no dad, oh my God!"

I could not cry. The other girl (Zainab) along with the 'new' mama (Ishatou) were both crying. I was thinking deeply why my father had never come to see me. Whereas, finally that night - that's when I cried! I continued to cry very often and would hide when I did as papa Sadou didn't want to see me so sad... I was 12 years old.

That first morning I awoke so sad and I have never forgotten that event. I would cry all over and again whenever I thought of my daddy and this lasted for a very long time.

Chapter 5: My Life In Conakry

It was two weeks later when the new mama, Ishatou, decided we all would go to my village of Kiri. Brother Yaya was there to meet us, but sister Aisha was not as she was living now in Senegal and was already married.

There was lots of crying, and talk of how my father missed me through all the years of my absence. Ishatou now got the letter given to her in which she and Seadou were not to allow my father's brother, Bobo to keep me. If in the event they did not want to keep me, then they were to return me to the others of my family in the village.

This made the 'Capital Family' happy as they did want to keep me; but they did allow me to stay with my brother Yaya for a few months before I returned to them.

The pleasant stepmother, Fatou, decided, with the death of my father, to go back to her own extended family, leaving some of her belongings and her small cabana to my still single, and talented, brother, who was a good cook and often cooked for the family after mother died.

*   *   *

I realized I would have to be better than before with Saidou and Ishatou or I might be sent back to Kiri and there was nothing left in this village for me anymore. The bigger problem was with the two nieces still living in the house, the younger was difficult and never helped with any chores and the older did so only rarely.

Saidou and Ishatou also had three other older boys who lived in the same city and visited often.

Saidou over-complimented me, calling me aside telling me how much he appreciated my effort. However he never saw to it that I got any relief. In the morning I would awake at six am: mop the house; sweep the porch; clean the dishes after breakfast; go to the market; and return with the food and cook it. There always were various chores for me after all this.

The other house working girl, Zainab, and I asked to be put in school but they only said they said they would think about it, but it never happened..

*   *   *

In Africa to talk back to any elder is not accepted and if you do they slap you and treat you badly. Then they often complain to the man of the house when he returns home and try to get you into trouble.

One day I remember working all day and the middle aged niece came into the bedroom at eleven pm while I was sleeping. She turned the light so I couldn't sleep so I would be tired the whole following day. I asked her,

"Please turn off the light as I have to start work early."

Her reply was, "No, you don't tell me what to do!"

She pulled me out of bed to the outside on the porch, and locked the house's outer-doors (so no one could get to us). She started hitting, slapping and choking me. I tried to defend myself but she was stronger. This tussle went on for about thirty minutes and gave me bruises on my face. In the morning I was sick with pain.

I did get up at the usual six am and seeing me, Ishatou urged me to explain what had happened. When the niece was confronted with what had been done to me, she said,

"She is lying!"

Then the family realized the truth and the 'mama,' told me,

"Don't touch her but come straight to me, okay?"

The abuse ceased as mama and papa put a stop to it.

*   *   *

I was around thirteen years old when I was given a project of learning how to do design embroidery. It took place every day, Monday through Friday and when the teaching was done I still had many chores to do. Because of the traffic and distance I did not get home until around six pm. This learning lasted one year and then the business closed, but now I have a skill.

Saidou had a daughter, Hassanatou, who lived in the United States and she came to Africa during my training period. She asked me one day,

"Why don't you learn hair work, that will be good for you?"

I thought this was a good idea and Ishatou thought so also and approached a local salon. So now I was developing another useful skill and Hassanatou remarked that it will be good for me one day and then she said,

"I think you are a good person."

One month later I started to go to the salon to learn. Every Friday and Saturday coming back from there I would go to study the Qu'rán for one hour. This Qua'ronic teacher would minister to a group of young people in his home. He did this for me without charge. In return I would do his laundry and sometimes I would bring him some food to eat.

The father was all for this idea because he said I was such a good worker in the house, and mama said,

"Whatever you want to learn is okay." In the end he and his daughter got support from mama for all this - but I was not to tell anybody about the arrangement until about three months or so later.

*   *   *

One day mama Ishatou said to me,

"We have an appointment, let's go."

"What kind, I asked?" but neither parent would tell me because of the family girls and merely replied they wanted to explain later.

I began to worry they were going to give me a husband and I was still only fourteen! So I started wearing old, bad looking clothes whenever I thought a prospective husband would show up. Then no one would want to marry me. I was asked,

"Why are you wearing such poor clothes?"

I responded, "My good clothes need washing."

*　　*　　*

In a short time we went to see a lady who turned out to be one who obtained passports. Again, I didn't know what was going on as mama and the lady sat on an inside sofa talking as I sat outside.

When they finished their discussion mama and I got into a rented car driven by a fellow who knew Ishatou quite well and he asked her,

"What are we doing here?"

Her answer rang back in my ears, "Oh, my Fatima is going to America," and I mentally thought, *oh I am so glad all this was not for a husband!*

I was so excited about going to the USA.

*   *   *

I asked Ishatou if I could go to the village and say goodby to my brother and grandma before leaving for America.

She said, "Yes, but don't let any of the girls know."

The mean younger one though heard the parents talking, letting the other girls know and later said to me,

"I think they are taking you somewhere, maybe to the USA. I'm leaving home and I'm not going to do all the work you do here!   So, before you leave I'm going home to my father's house."

Chapter 6: A Long Journey Begins

All three girls in the house asked me over and over where I was going and I told them,

"I don't know."

This was really because Ishatou said I was not to tell anyone They all found out anyway and then got so upset and said to me,

"Why do you have to go and not us?"

So, I said, "I don't know."

Ishatou was scared of me going to my village to say goodbye to the family. I asked why. She said your dad's brother, who now lives in Kiri, will try and give you a husband.

Realizing this I was scared too, but I replied,

"I really want to see grandma Oumou, and my brother Yaya, because I don't know if I'll ever come back to see them again."

Papa Saidou said, "Don't worry I will give you a letter to give to my close friend, Omar, who lives in the market there. He is a very important man, like a chief leader and will see it gets to your dad's brother, Bobo. The inside of the letter read: *Fatima only comes to "Hi," to her family. She is going to the United States. She does not want to get married.*

This letter was to stay with Omar. He intended to send someone with it to tell Bobo he must send me back to the village market place to Chief Omar

*   *   *

I went to Kiri and found out that my brother Yaya had moved to Gambia. So I asked my stepmother, "Where is my brother?"

She said, "I don't know."

The next morning I went to see grandma and asked, "What happened?"

Oumou turned her head my way and started crying, finally saying,

"Do you remember the farm and everything before you left?"

"Yes."

"Isha, your sister, also got a divorce from her young husband because they were too young and didn't get along. Then Bobo told her she could not stay in Kiri and he gave her to an old, mean guy for a husband even though she didn't want him! And now she is miserable.

"Your stepmother and Bobo took everything away from Yaya, and Bobo and the widow, the two of them, got married and now control everything. So your brother was left with nothing and went away. But the parents of Yaya's very close friend, Marianna, asked him to marry her and gave them a bit of money to leave the country and they went to Gambia."

I went to the stepmother and Bobo and directly asked why they had taken everything away from my brother and they began yelling and screaming at me. Bobo said,

"You are 14 years old and you are going to get married and not go back to the capital."

Now I was really scared and thought, *what am I going to do now? Should I run away and take a bus back to Conakry on my own?"*

Bobo had three sons at home and told them to watch me closely. But then Omar had finally sent a message to Bobo that demanded he come to the market place and meet with him. Bobo asked why Omar wanted to see him and the reply from the messenger was,

"I don't know!"

Omar had much power in this area since he was an elder; devoutly read and quoted the Qur'án; and possibly because he owned the land area on which the market rested. Bobo, before leaving for the market, told one of his sons he would have to choose me or another girl from Kiri (both of us being present) as a wife.

The son replied,

"Remember daddy, I married a 12 year old pregnant wife and she and the baby died. And now you want me to marry another young girl? I am not ready to get married again!"

Bobo merely said, "When I get back we will talk about it!"

     * * *

Bobo met with Omar and it was explained that Fatima had only come to say goodbye to her family and now she was going to the USA to have a better life!

Bobo said, "No, I don't want her to go."

Omar insisted, "She is going to go!"

Bobo relented, and said, "I will let her go for a little while."

The chief responded, "Okay, that's good."

     * * *

Bobo returned to the village later and asked me,

"Oh, you are going to the United States?"

I said, "Yes."

"How long will you be in the USA?"

I told him, "One year."

He said, "You better come back in one year!"

"All right, I will come back in one year."

Finally, I reflected, *I think I'm on my way to the USA. The nightmare is over.*

Chapter 7: Prayers Are Sometimes Answered

After I had first returned from Kiri to the capital, Ishatou had asked,

"How was your trip to see the family?"

"I told her and papa what happened with the farm and to my brother and how they took everything away from Yaya."

I then related Yaya's marriage to his dear friend Marianna and how the two of them had moved to Gambia. I also told of my sister Isha's divorce from her young husband, as they didn't get along, and her following forced remarriage to a local, very mean, elderly man.

I also told them of Bobo's effort to get me a husband, as I thought, *I am so glad papa gave Omar the letter to protect me.*

I then informed them that Bobo intended me for his middle son. But the son spoke up saying to his papa,

"Remember you had me marry my wife of 12 years of age and she and the baby died in childbirth and I refuse to marry Fatima or anyone else so young!"

The couple on hearing this said,

"We are happy you have come back."

*   *   *

Ishatou had one nephew, Salou. When he was nineteen and I was ten years old, one day I was washing my hands and I accidentally splashed water on his face as I was drying them and he slapped me really hard causing my face to swell up.

I complained to his mother about what happened and she just insisted I just let it go and wash all his clothes anyway.

I saids, "I cannot do that!"

Her reply was, "You have to do it or you will be whipped!"

So, I did it.

*   *   *

Hassnatou's husband came to Africa alone to visit all the family but she stayed back in America during this trip.

One morning he came to me and said,

"We are going to see someone who will get you a passport."

Now, I was very, very excited. Unfortunately, all the girls in the house were jealous of my good fortune.

There were now a lot of arguments about who would do all the housework when I was gone. Soon I was taken by the sister of Nasar's, (Hassnatou's husband) to the US Embassy to request a visa. I was quite nervous about this and I prayed all night that I would be the one or two out of a hundred who would be chosen to receive a visa to America.

I clearly remember a white lady interviewer who was responsible for giving out such a visa as she inquired,

"How long will you stay in the USA?"

I said, "I am just going for a little while."

She then asked about my parents and I told her they were both dead and her response was, "I'm sorry to hear that. Then you are going for a vacation?"

I thought it best to just say, "Yes."

"Okay, hand me your passport and we will let you know."

I was anxious and said,

"Madam, please, I beg your help to get me there!"

"We certainly will let you know within a week from now."

I answered simply, "Thank you."

On my way out of the building I saw people crying because apparently their conversations about getting a visa had not gone well. I told myself,

I will continue to pray on it - I know it is going to work for me!

*   *   *

As promised, I received my answer at the end of the week. It was while I was sitting at home, when one of the uncles came in who had an envelope in his hand! He said, with a slight smile,

"I have good news for you!'

"What good news do you have?"

"That you are so lucky to have this - I was looking for this for 10 years, but never got it!"

I said, still not fully realizing what good luck this was,

"What is it?"

"Your passport and visa is here."

I opened the passport and saw the official Visa.

I was so happy ... my prayers were answered!

Chapter 8: Getting Ready To Go

Ishatou wasn't home when my visa arrived and neither was Saedou. When they did return I told them about the visa.

The two asked to see it and exclaimed,

"Oh, you are so lucky to have gotten it," and mama added, "remember don't tell anyone about it or let them see the passport. In fact, Fatima handed the passport to me, for safekeeping.

*   *   *

The next morning Hassnatou called from America and was told I now had my visa. She was excited and informed us

"I am going to tell my best friend, who is in Guinea and coming to the US so that she can travel with Fatima. I'll find out about the tickets and buy them."

The following morning Ishatou took me to her mother's house and explained to her I had received my visa. She also requested the mother to talk to me, reminding me to be very nice, not talk back to my elders and behave better than I have done before.

Of course . . . I promised to be very nice to everyone!

When Ishatou and I returned home papa said,

"Now I need to speak to you, Fatima."

He reminded me a few years before, when I was 12 years old, the local army base had a big munitions explosion; it was while I was at the market. I clearly recalled this. Everyone around me started running away from the base area. I was so scared and I ran too. But I knew papa had lost sight in his left eye and had some difficulty in his right because of glaucoma.

I decided to go home and found out all the family had run away and Ishatou was busy helping for her mother too, so I went to papa and said,

"Let's go as everyone has run away. I will help you, so give me your hand"

I got his clothes ready and to make him feel safe told him,

"I will not let go of your hand papa, I promise."

*   *   *

The exploding vibrations were felt all over and surrounding the house yet papa Saidou would not leave. He held my hand and soon calmed me down. Finally, everyone in the family got home and told us that many of the fleeing people got injured and a few killed and staying in the house was the safest thing to do.

[According to the Archives of the U.S. State Department, in addition to many people being injured, ten people lost their lives when the ammunition depot, at the Conakry military base, erupted, setting off a series of explosions and a large fire.]

Then papa began to cry and said,

"Everyone ran away except Fatima, she stayed to look after me. She is a good girl. I will never forget about this."

A short time later papa gave me his 'little advice,'

"Fatima you are a good and nice girl, please never change. Be as nice or even nicer when you get to America and respect your elders. I will pray for you and you will be blessed forever!"

*   *   *

Two weeks later Hassnatou's friend, Ama planned to return to the US from Africa and was asked if he would bring me with him. His answer was yes!

Every day I prayed that this day would come, and I thought, *I will work even harder when I get to America. I plan to then help my sister and brother by sending them some money and also this family who have raised me.*

*   *   *

Monday morning Hassnatou called and had said,

"I have got the ticket for Fatima. She is to come with my friend, Ama. He is returning to Dallas, where he lives."

Mama said, "Fatima is ready to go and she is going to be very happy."

"Well then,"responded their daughter, "go ahead and tell her the good news"

Mama informed me and then the rest of the family, "You will leave at 2 pm next Wednesday."

On hearing all this I reflected, *My prayers were answered again, Oh God, thank you!*

Tuesday morning I went to mama and papa to talk to them,

"Thank you," then I started crying, "I am so sorry if I ever did anything to displease you or by doing bad while I lived here. I know raising a child is not easy, but you did raise and helped me."

They started to cry also and papa said,

"You are a good girl. We have raised a lot of young girls here but we have never seen anyone like you. This is why we agreed to let you go and have a better life."

"Okay, thank you for teaching me so many things including allowing me to develop the skills by working in a hair salon and later in the technique of beading design.

They said, "You are welcome - you will stay blessed as always."

Now everybody cried.

*   *   *

The next day I would be leaving for good and I felt very happy.

I said to myself, *I prayed for this and finally the day has arrived!*

I went to do my hair and got back to the house and dressed before going to the airport with a contented smile on my face. I said goodbye to everyone.

At the check-in area I gave my passport to the counter lady. The funny thing was the processing was taking so long - and now I was getting scared - time to pray again, *Please God, do not return me back here in Africa. I have gotten so far.*

Finally the computer worked.

I got my passport handed to me and now I breathed freely and was happy again. The lady told us to wait in the seating area and so we did.

Another thing: I lost my paper with my seat number on it.

"Oh no!" I started to sweat. I went back to praying. Ama saw me doing this and he asked, "What's wrong!"

"I lost the number to my seat. Am I going to stay here?"

He relieved me by saying, "No, you won't."

Chapter 9: A Dream Comes True

Ama suggested, "Keep looking, the seat slip may be inside your passport."

So, I looked carefully and indeed found it in the passport book and now, I am happy again; I am on my way.

*   *   *

We boarded and found our seats. I was so excited being in the plane - it was the first time for me. I looked around and found everything was so clean and said to myself, *I cannot believe this is really happening to* me, *I never, ever imagined actually being in an airplane. I'm going to America where everybody wants to go, but few are able to get a visa. And in addition, I skipped having to get married at age fourteen.*

Then the tears started coming into my eyes. Ama looked at me and commented,

"Why are you crying, Fatima?"

"Oh, I'm just so happy."

"Don't cry, you will be fine and will like America."

Finally the plane took off just as night fell. By morning we landed in Brussel, Belgium. It was so unusual to see so many white people and so many planes. I had been so worked up I hadn't slept at all on the flight.

Ama said, "Now we deplane and wait for the second flight, on to the US. Don't you want to take a nap, Fatima?"

I answered, "No, I am not sleepy, just filled with excitement"

"All right, I will take a nap and you can watch our bags."

A short time later he awoke and said, "Let me find something for us to eat."

He came back shortly with some croissants which I had never tasted before and they were very good. In fact, I started to put the left-overs in my pack and Ama said,

"No, not necessary, there will be food in the next plane."

"So, I can't take them to the US?"

"No, Fatima, there are lots of them in that country."

"Are you sure because they are so good?"

Ama laughed, "Yes, I am absolutely sure."

*　　*　　*

The next flight was on time so we quickly boarded it.

I am now in a contented state because we have finished the first step of the journey. But when the plane taxied
onto the tarmac, raved up its engines, rolled down the take
off strip, and roared and vibrated a lot as my mood changed
from happiness to a bit scared. So, of course, I started praying.

Eleven hours later we landed at the Dallas Fort Worth
Airport in Texas. Hassanatou's husband, Nasar, was working at the DFW airport, moving baggage from the planes to
the claim pick up areas in a motorized cart. He came directly
into the plane and called out,

"Fatima, you are here."

We were both happy to see each other and hugged.
Then he said he would get my bags for me. Next we had to
pass through security and we were asked,

"Why do you come to the United States?"

Nasar translated for me and informed me, "She
comes to visit."

The guard stamped my papers for a six month stay.

Nasar then said to me, "Fatima, let's go home. Hassanatou and the three kids are waiting for you."

*   *   *

We got 'home' around one pm and everyone seemed excited to meet me. After all the greetings were exchanged I took a shower and ate with them. Now I thought, *It was time to pray to God and thank Him for all these things that had come about.* That accomplished, I slept very soundly until seven am the next morning. At breakfast I was asked how everyone back home was and I had to say all were happy for me except for the girls. Then I asked,

"Can you call papa Saidou and Ishatou so I can speak to them?"

So we called them, and I told them I'm eating well here!"

They exclaimed, "Good for you, we are happy for you."

So we signed off because we were using a calling card and we were out of time.

*   *   *

Because it was at the end of summer vacation I got to play a lot with the children. It was then that Hassanatou came to me and stated,

"The children will shortly be going back to school. Do you want to go to school too, Fatima?"

"That is my dream!"

"Okay, we will go to the school and talk to the councilor."

*   *   *

In the councilor's interview I had to admit I did not know any English. Then she said,

"We will put you in ESL (English as a Second Language) classes."

"That would be good," responded Hassanatou," because she was not allowed to go to school in her own country."

It was one week later I started my class. The first day I met the teacher, Marie; she didn't speak French and I didn't speak English! When we were introduced I could not understand her words but by looking closely at her and especially her motions I picked up that she was introducing herself to me. So I spoke out, "Marie."

She said, "Yes, yes, Marie, that's right!"

I was pleased with this understanding since I had never been to a school.

So, not knowing how to say my name in English ... I tapped on my chest and repeated my name, "Fatima, Fatima."

She handed me some paper and a pencil and made me know I should write my name and so I did. It was back in

Guinea that I knew a neighbor who was a teacher and he taught me a little reading and writing in French. He would tell me I was smart and he would tutor me. I would have to sneak out of the house so none of the family would know about this, and never told them.

Marie was impressed with my writing skill. I was to continue to go to the ESL classes for the next three years, greatly learning and expanding my English vocabulary.

*   *   *

During this schooling time I met two sisters in the class who were from the country of Dijbouti and fluent in French. The three of us easily understood each other. Their dad had brought them to America. Even more helpful, they had learned some English at a school in their home country.

They helped me a lot in class. Soon we all became the best of friends. Their mother was living in Canada but planned to come to the US quite soon. Their father would bring them to my new home so the three of us could 'hang out.'

About once a week Hassanatou and I would call Isha-tou and Saidou in Africa. On an early call they asked how things were going.

I answered, "This is a beautiful place and there is good food. Also there are lots of trees and fine roads." Then I added, "I am going to school here!"

They responded, "Oh, wow! That's wonderful, you are a smart girl. Good Luck!"

"Okay" I responded, "thank you guys for letting me come here."

"You are very welcome, Fatima."

I asked how Sadou's nieces and Zeinab were doing and ended saying,

"Please say hi to them for me."

*   *   *

One day Hassanatou's best friend came for a visit and while she was there gave me 20 dollars. I asked how much money this was in Guinea francs. She said, "25,000 francs."

"Oh," I exclaimed, "that's a lot in Africa. Can I send the money to Ishatou and Saidou?"
"Oh no," Hassanatou answered, "just keep it."

"No please, let me send it, everything good that has happened to me is because of those two."

So I received a promise that the money would be sent and Hassanatou would call them and tell them it was coming.

Saidou, when told of this, asked where the money came from and he was told.

To this, he responded, "I can't imagine Fatima being able to send this money as she just got there. That was a nice thing for the friend to do, and also tell Fatima thank you, you are going to be blessed."

Then he signed off by saying goodbye.

*   *   *

Hassanatou's kids and I were hanging out a lot now; we like going to restaurants and all kinds of activities together and I kept reminding myself, *I love America.*

One day Hassanatou told me, "My friend has a salon, so let's go there and see if you can work a little bit."

I went there and the lady tested me for one hour and remarked, in French,
"Oh, you are very good. Can you come in once a week, on the weekend, and work here." Then she gave me forty dollars and I thought, "*back home this would be a lot! Maybe I'll send it to my sister, Isha, remembering the last time I saw her in Kiri and how she was suffering with her present husband. She had wanted to cook me a meal of good food but she could not afford it and asking her husband for some money he gave her so little it was not possible.*"

(During this time - 2005, the rate of exchange for one US dollar was approximately around 5000 Francs. Today's rates vary around 9,650).

My sister Isha had been worried over this, so I had calmed her down and told her,

"I will help you someday. I am going to America."
Then I asked, "Do you have any information about Yaya?"

She answered, "No, I don't"

"Isha, I miss him."

She responded, "Me too."

*   *   *

I was able at that time to spend three days with her before I returned to Conakry. I was now in the US and 16 years old when all this memory had come back to me as the salon lady gave me the 40 dollars. So I said to Hassanatou,

"Let me send this money to my sister in Africa."

She asked, "Why don't you save your money?"

"You don't understand?"

"Fatima, what is it I don't understand; talk to me, please."
"My sister is married to an old man who has some money but he only gives her very little and if I send this money it will be 50,000 francs! That will help him a lot."

Hassanatou agreed and added, "Let's send this to your sister and how about we find you a little job?"

"Yes, that would be wonderful."

"So what is it you would like to do?"

"Any kind of job would be okay."

"How about baby-sitting some of my friend's children and once a week going to the salon, that way you can send some and keep some money?"

"Okay, let's do that."

Chapter 10: A Courting We Will Go

Twice a week I started baby sitting and going to school on Tuesday and Wednesday for two hours. On the weekends I worked at the salon and I could make forty or fifty dollars along with sitting for the two children. I kept 30.00 dollars for myself and sent 70.00 to help back home.

One day, out of nowhere, my brother, Yaya called.

I answered and asked,

"Who is this ?"

He said, "Yaya, is this Fatima?"

"Yes."

"It's me, your brother!"

I started shaking and crying, as he managed to say,

"Oh, Are you crying, Fatima?" and he started to cry.

I asked him, "How did you get this number, Yaya?"

"I asked so many people and finally papa Saidou and he gave it to me."

"How are you doing over there, Yaya?"

"I'm okay now but I have suffered a lot."

"What happened to you? I went to Kiri to say goodbye to you but you had left."

Our dad's brother tried to do bad things to me, so I went away. They had taken everything from me so I had to go. I have a wife now and a baby."

What kind of baby?"

"A girl: Awa."

"I am happy for you, Yaya. Okay, we will talk much longer; I see your number, so hang up and let me call you back on my phone card. Okay,"

 And that's what I did and told him of my little jobs.

"Oh, lucky you!"

"Yes, and best of all, I skipped getting married."

"Wow, I knew they would try to do that to you."

 Before I signed off I made a promise, "Yaya, I will send you some money"

He was happy to hear that and later I sent him $100 dollars, which helped him a lot!

*   *   *

Not long after this papa Saidou called Hassanatou about me and told her,

"I want one of my nephews to marry Fatima."

She replied, "That's what you want; you want them to marry right now?"

"Yes, she is eighteen now. Talk to Fatima then I will call her later."

So Hassanatou told me. I responded to her,

"Oh no, I only met him once in Conakry when we were both young. Okay I'll talk to papa, in fact I will call him now. But Hassanatou, how can I marry someone who is not even here?"

*   *   *

"I'm glad you called me, Fatima. I wish you to marry my nephew, Amar - please do not say no."

I said, "Papa, how can I marry someone who doesn't live in the US, but lives in Spain?"

"Yeah, I know that, but I still want you to marry him. He will come to you later."

In my mind I said, *I don't want this, in fact I don't even like him, but I can't say no to papa Saidou.*

What I did say to papa, because I did not want to disappoint him was,

"Okay, let me talk to Ishatou.

"Yes, yes, she is right here ..."

"Fatima, he is a good guy and you have to marry him!"

"No, I don't want to, mama.'

"Please, please, Fatima, marry him!"

My last response was,

"I will call you back later," and I hung up.

*   *   *

I was upset and crying. Then the guy, Amar, calls from Spain. The first call I didn't answer so I got a voicemail,

"Oh, Fatima, I'll call you back this afternoon," And he did!

"Fatima, they have told me all about you, I think I want to get married to you!" I'm pretty sure I want to get married to you."

"Well, I'm not sure about how I feel about that."

"Please think about it."

"I will."

"Good, I'll call you back in three days, all right?"

"Okay, Amar."

*   *   *

But in two days time papa called again and asked about Amar, saying,

"He called, right?"

"Yes, but I don't want to marry him!"

"Fatima, don't say that."

"What do you want me to say, papa?"

"I just want you to say yes; he will be very good for you."

"Okay ... I will marry him!"

This made everyone happy ... except me.

*   *   *

Papa and Mama planned the whole wedding back home in Africa; they got everything ready; and I got married!

But not in person! Amar was still in Spain and I was in the US. Later in that afternoon of the ceremony Amar and then papa and mama called me to give their congratulations. I was told the festivities were very good with a lot of people, good food and many presents of clothes.

However nothing was legally signed. The instructions given to Amar was to get a visa to the US so he could join his quasi wife!

Chapter 11:
How The Situation Of This Marriage Now Stands

Well, I'm married; what have I done to myself? Now because it's done I have to deal with this for the rest of my life. I should have just said no but we have the customs I have been raised in. I never said no to them whatever they asked, and that is the only reason I agreed to this.

But ... I live in the US now and though I no longer have to do everything asked of me, I do because that's what I did in Africa. I know exactly what to do now; it is time to pray to God again and He will help solve this problem right away as everyone is always congratulating me on the marriage.

I must remind myself, Fatima, it is going to be okay, I mean it's going to be four years before Amar even gets his documented papers from Spain before he can come to the US. So, God, that gives us time to work this out. However Amar is calling me all the time now. We talk about a lot of things.

Also my sister recently called me and asked,

"Do you want to go to Spain, Fatima?"

"No, I do not, Aisha. Every day I keep praying and say to God, 'You have answered my prayers before and will again,' and He will."

"Yet, Amar is calling almost every day now and just asked me questions like what kind of clothes and shoes I like. I said, I don't need anything Amar."

To which he replied, "But you are my wife!"

"Yeah," I said, "I will let you know if I need anything."

To which he stated, "Okay, and how are you doing over there, Fatima?"

"Very well."

"You like the US?"

"Yes, Amar, I like it."

"What about Spain?"

"I don't know, Amar."

"It's nice here too. I can't wait to see you!"

"Amar, let's talk tomorrow, I am tired today."

"Yes, Thank you and goodbye, Fatima."

That sounded so strange, am I really a wife?

*   *   *

The next morning my dad's brother, Bobo, called,

"It's me, Bobo. How are you, Fatima?"

"Fine - I'm okay."

"You told me you were coming back to Africa."

"Yeah, I didn't want to come back!"

"Oh, so you tricked me."

"Yes, I did."

"Why did you do that?"

"I don't know, what you did was not good."

"Fatima, I did nothing wrong."

"You tried to give me your son as a husband at a very young age, something neither of us wanted."

"Yet it was the right thing to do."

I firmly said, "It was not!"

"If your dad was alive he would have wanted the same thing."

"No, my dad loved me, my sister and my brother very much and he would not do that to us. And I miss him so much. I have too much going on in my life right now and nobody to talk to about it, except Hassanatou."

Then Bobo said, "I went to Conakry, and Saidou and Ishatou told me about Amar, the guy you just married. I also saw the doctor in the capital because I am sick and he told me I can't make it!"

"I am sorry to hear that, Bobo."

"Do you like Amar?"

"Yes."

"Why did you run away from my son?"

"I didn't want to marry him - that's why."

"Well, you ended up marrying someone."

"Yes, I did. If daddy was still alive all of this would never have happened."

"Okay, I will let you go now, Fatima."

"Thank you and goodbye"

One month later Bobo died!

*   *   *

Amar sent me 200 Euros from Spain a bit after this and I said to my sister,

"I don't think I want to use this money."

She replied, "Yes, but this guy is married to you so you have to use it because he eventually will join you in the US."

*   *   *

While in America I never had a boyfriend. If asked, "Are you married?"

I would say, "Yes, I am," because if I didn't, sometimes I would be requested to go out with them. I began to feel I would have to learn to love Amar before the next three years were up. So, first I went to the store, spent my money, not the money he had sent me, (which I sent to the family in Africa). I bought him some clothes and mailed them to him in Spain.

He was so happy about this that he sent me a photograph of himself dressed up in this gift. He asked me to send a photo of myself and so we knew exactly how we presently looked to each other.

Over this time papa would call and say things like, "Don't worry, Amar will join you soon."

*   *   *

Souieymane, the son of my not so nice stepmother, Saratou, is now a grown man. He is planning on getting married. His problem is he doesn't have enough money for the marriage. So, they decided to call me and my sister and brother to help. Saratou called me first.

I asked, "Who is calling?"

It's me, Saratou, how are you?"

I responded, "I'm okay."

Her tone of voice acted as if nothing bad had taken place between us. She stated, "Your stepbrother, Souieymane, is a big man now, Fatima, and he is going to get married. And oh, we need you guys to help."

I asked her, "Did you call Yaya?"

"Not yet. I wished first to talk to you. You remember how I love you all so much; the same as my own kids."

"Yes. You do remember what you did to my brother and sister!"

"It wasn't my decision."

"No, you and Bobo *both* did that. If you do these bad things, life doesn't last too long."

"Don't say that Fatima, we're a family."

"Oh, so now we're a family! Well, I miss my true mom and my dad so much; they both passed too soon."

"I have decided to call you for help."

"What kind of help, Saratou?"

"We don't have enough money for Souieymane's wedding."

"Okay, now you have to call my brother Yaya?"

"I will try Fatima, goodbye for now."

*   *   *

Not hearing back from Saratou, I called Yaya later and asked him,

"Did Saratou call you?"

"No Fatima, she did not call."

So I told him about our stepbrother's coming marriage and the family's need for our financial help. Yaya responded in a negative way,

"I don't think that is a good idea,"

"But he is our half brother who really needs the help, and anyway you don't have the money for that and neither does our sister, Aisha. So I will help."

"Oh sister, is that what you want to do?"

"Yes. When someone is mean to you, don't return the meanness in kind. I do not have a lot of money but I will share what I have. I'll send three hundred US dollars to you and then you send it to Saratou from the three of us. It should amount to around three million Guinea Francs, which is a lot In Africa."

(The usual way to start a transfer of funds to family members in Africa is a transfer in US dollars: from a debit/credit card or money from your online banking account; the transfer agent will charge a fair market exchange rate; the monies are locally delivered; in this case to the market agent for the village of Kiri; and it is personally pick up by the family recipient).

"Wow, Fatima, you are a good sister and I will do it."

I soon got another and more excited call from Saratou,

"Fatima, thank you, thank you; the money will help your half brother a lot, you are a good person."

Chapter 12: Married I Can Always Get

Approximately three and a half years passed until Amar got his documents to come to the US. When they did arrive he called to let me know.

I told him, "I'm happy for you, we will meet soon. I will start looking for an apartment for us."

Without any further conversation on this subject he merely said,

"Okay, we will talk about it."

And we both said, "Good bye for now."

Papa Saidou called the very next day and confirmed to me,

"Your husband will be coming very shortly."
This I acknowledged, saying, "Okay papa, we will talk again soon," and we hung up.

*   *   *

It was a week later when Amar called again, and he abruptly asked,

"We need to talk! Where were you yesterday?"

"I went to the mall with a friend."

"I don't like you going out so much, because you are my wife."

"I went with my girlfriend from school," I reported.

"I still don't like it."

"Amar, you know, since we got married you try to control everything I do!"

"Of course, I do that because you are my wife."

"Well, I don't want to have that kind of life!"

Leaving the subject at hand he said,

"Anyway, did my uncle call you?"

"Yes, he did."

"He also called me and told me I need to go to the US now. But I told him, no, Fatima needs to come to Spain. He said you could not as you don't have the documents to do that. So, I told him I will try to go to America then."

That was the up-in-the-air end of that conversation.

*   *   *

The following week I called Amar back and told him the cost of the apartment rental would be five hundred dollars a month and he quickly replied,

"That's too much."

"Don't worry about it, I will take care of it for now."

He next addressed the departure and arrival subject,

"Fatima, In three months I will be coming to see you."

Based on this commitment and remark, I added,

"All right, I'll start buying the furniture."

I discussed this recent conversation that Amar and I had with Hassanatou and she offered,

"We will start getting things for the apartment," and I agreed with her.

Now everyone was excited over Amar's soon arrival. Amar and I talked many times during these next two months. And papa called him to confirm the exact date asking,

"Amar, are you finally ready to go to America?"

A weak answer was returned,

"Uncle, I don't think I want to go right now."

This was not the response papa was looking for and he yelled at him,

"Don't think, get up and go. This girl has been waiting for you over the last four years and a lot of people wanted to marry her but she was married to you."

"Okay, uncle, I will call you back tomorrow."

Papa accepted this delay and merely said sharply, "All right!"

Back in Spain, Amar was most probably in deep thought throughout the night about what he should do. What he did was call his older brother in Africa and asked for a favor.

"What kind of favor do you want, Amar?"

Go see Uncle Saidou and tell him I do not want to go to the US. And I no longer want to be married to Fatima anymore."

"What! You have to tell that to uncle yourself, I don't have the kind of mouth to do it."

"Okay, forget it, I will do it myself."

*   *   *

The very next day the call to the man was made,

"Uncle, how are you? I want to tell you something."
With a possible tone of suspicion in his voice, the uncle answered,

"Okay, go ahead, Amar."

"I have been thinking deeply, I do not want to go to the US and ... I don't want to stay married to Fatima!"

"What!"

"That's what I have decided."

"Why are you doing this to her, she has organized everything - you are going to America!"

"She should have come to me."

"You know without documents she cannot come to Spain."

"Yeah, I know, but that is what I want."

"You, Amar, are going to call Fatima and tell her all this, I am not going to do it!"

"I will, uncle, goodbye."

*   *   *

The promised call came to me that night,

"Hello, Fatima."

"Hi, Amar. Guess what, I got some nice stuff for the apartment, I'll pick it up a little later. Let's see, it is only a couple more weeks and you will be here. Hello ... you seem very quiet tonight. Are you tired?"

"No, I need to talk to you."

"What's up, is something wrong?"

"I don't want to leave Spain. All my friends are here and they tell me don't leave the country. You can have a wife here."

"What are you saying Amar?"

"It's not because of ladies. I just don't want to remain married to you and don't want to come to the US."

"Oh my gosh, did you hear what you just said to me?"

"Yeah."

"Well, it's night here, I will call you tomorrow."

'Okay."

Through the sleepless night I wondered if something was mentally wrong with him and I felt it was best to wait until morning to see if his thinking was more clear.

I did call him in the morning and asked,

"How are you now?"

"I'm good, Fatima. What I told you last night is what I really want. You know, I don't drink, I don't smoke and my mind is okay and what I said last night is exactly what I want!"

"Okay Amar ... you could have told me this a bit earlier. So I will say goodbye!"

"Goodbye, Fatima."

I hung up and began to cry ... a lot. Hassanatou found me like this and asked,

"What is wrong, what is the matter?"

"Amar cut off the marriage."

"Are you serious?"

"I am serious, yes."

"Don't cry over this, you can get a good husband here, a better one."

*   *   *

The next day Amar called Hassanatou and discussed his decision about me.

Hassanatou asked twice, "Is this what you really want?"

His reply was brief, "Yes, it is."

To which her answer was to the point,

"Okay, Amar, thank you and goodbye."

*   *   *

(In Islam the term Talag is commonly translated as "repudiation" meaning divorce. It refers to the husband's right to dissolve the marriage by:
    * simply announcing to his wife his desire
    * though most Muslims do not encourage divorce
    * generally remarrying is permitted
    * marriage however is a contract to live together

Sunni Muslims do not encourage divorce but permit it if the marriage has broken down. The husband must express his desire on divorce three times over a period of 3 months.

Shi'ah Muslims require at least two witnesses followed by a period before the marriage ends.

When a woman initiates a divorce it is called a Kula and there is a waiting period to ensure there is no pregnancy.

There are significant pressures in not going through a divorce: the contract is said to be made before God and is supposed to be for life; extended families also play a vital role in helping with the issues; the Mahr, which is the amount of monies given to the bride: is hers to spend as she pleases. Also the Inman in the mosque can be asked by either or both parties to help with any other issues and the local customs can often bring many other items of restraint).

So, it is no easy thing to get a divorce!

Chapter 13: It's Not Over Until It's Over

I cried a bit but Hassanatou asked me please not to do it, saying,

"Everything will turn out okay and I will help. I can't believe, Fatima, he would do this to you after waiting all this time"

I was nonetheless still very upset and cried on and off for another week. Then papa called

"Hi Fatima, how are you, all right? Did Amar call you?"

"Yes, he did. He said he decided he didn't really want to come to the US. I think his friends are the ones who decided this course for him."

"He certainly could have told you sooner. You are a very good girl, Fatima, and I am most sorry for all this. I put you in all this mess, again I am very sorry."

"Okay papa; I have to tell you I really never wanted to marry him from the very first. I did cry a lot over it but there was no one with whom I could discuss the problem."

"Oh no! ... You will be blessed by God for the way you handled this!"

*   *   *

Well, I prayed to God and asked his support and tried to learn to love the man. Everybody was calling me to find out what happened and why he did this. They also called Amar and he began to feel guilty. In addition, his dad was furious, and these pressures caused him to call Nasar again and tell him,

"Please, I want my wife back and I need your help!"

Nasar's response was, "Why did you do it in the first place?"

He answered, "I don't know, but I am sorry now."

*   *   *

In fact, Nasar did make a call to me and wanted to review all his previous discussions with Amar, but I quickly told him,

"No! It's over!"

To me everything was finally settled. Yet after all this, Amar had the unbelievable lack of feelings to call once again, beginning the conversation,

"Fatima, I believe you have been crying a lot and ..."

I cut him off and retorted,

"I am just fine now."

In a strange tone in his voice he responded,

"I know I did wrong and I want you back".

"Amar ... do not call me anymore, ever - it's over - au revoir!"

Chapter 14: Those Interested Can Form A Line

Two months later, it occurred to me, *I'm twenty years old now and I will fully decide things for myself!*

And guess what? Hassanatou gets a call from Ishatou who had another helpful suggestion saying,

"I've been thinking, why doesn't Fatima marry her cousin who lives in the United States?"

"Mom, please, the last relationship, as you remember, did not work out, do you really think you want to start this all over again?"

The mother admitted, "You're right."

So, at last the 'word is on the street,' that Fatima is fully free.

*　　*　　*

The state of being fully free seems not to define being totally free from the world and always in complete control of all things.

I had a long time friend in Dallas who was a very good friend, and we have remained friends to this day. Well, he now called me about his friend, Amadou in Austin and asked if this friend could phone me and introduce himself to me.

I decided to allow it and the call came shortly later. After he identified himself he directly said,

"I'm looking for a wife."

I carefully replied, "Well, that is something I will have to deeply think about."

He said, "Don't rush, it is not for now I just wanted you to know what I was really calling about."

(As is well known, usually in Islamic societies there is no western type of dating, unless the families are involved; that is, there are no blind dates).

We talked a little and he promised to call me back .

*   *   *

Hassanatou had another friend that had the dilemma of finding a wife for a brother. And if that wasn't enough a third guy from our monthly Family Union Community called me (similar story, different line) and we pleasantly talked and then he said,

"Hi, My name is Osman and my brother gave me your number. I wanted to talk with you sometime, is it okay if I call again?"

"Yeah, of course," I responded and since he didn't actually mention he wanted me as a wife, I didn't volunteer anything of importance, even though we talked a number of times.

(Our Family Union Community group is an Islamic cornerstone of family life and a society building block. It usually meets once a month for charity and celebration activities: like births, marriages or giving a helping hand to those that need it).

*   *   *

There was something that happened at this time. A lady who came from Africa to the US, who was related to Nasar, had stopped in Austin and visited a family there for a short time. This lady on learning Nasar was now in Dallas decided to visit that city and meet with him and Hassanatou.

Nasar asked, "So you came from Austin?"

She replied, "Yes." To which Hassanatou mentioned

"My sister is presently talking to a guy who lives in Austin."

"What is his name?" the visitor asked.

"His name is Amadou."

"Okay, Hassanatou, when I get back to Austin I will find out about him."

She did indeed do this by asking around in the family she originally stayed with when she first immigrated to the US, if by chance they knew of him. Surprisingly, they were familiar with Amadou. Therefore, they gave him a call and invited him to the house. They put a number of questions to him concerning me which included,

"Do you know a Fatima in Dallas?"

He admitted it saying, "I am talking to her on the phone but I haven't met her yet."

He was informed by this lady, "I spent three days with her; she is a very good girl and you should go and meet her."

Thus Amadou now became more excited to come to Dallas right away.

This led the lady to call Hassanatou back and say, "I met with Amadou, and the family also told me, he is a very, very good guy."

Hassanatou finally suggested I ask Amadou to come to Dallas so all of us could meet with him and we would know what both of us looked like. That's what I did.

*   *   *

Two weeks later Amadou did come to Dallas. He came with three friends, one of which one, Ahmed, introduced Amadou to me. We had made a lot of food to welcome the four.

I decided to be natural (without make up or dressy clothes). I did not want him to like the 'outer package,' instead of just the 'me.'

So Hassanatou said, "You have the interest of three men now, and remember my friend told me about her brother and so you can look at these guys and see who is the best."

* * *

Amadou did come to Dallas. At the time I was in my upstairs bedroom when the four came into the living room and I was a bit scared to meet them. Finally I overcame my shyness and descended the stairs, in my 'natural' clothes. He had come with three friends, and one of his friends did our personal introduction.

Thus we met, sat down, and surrounded by the families, both his and mine, talked of many things. After discussions of length, Amadou said his family would get back to us. Before this we ate BBQ Chicken, rice, beef soup and a mixed salad; followed up by a dessert of fruit cake with ginger juice. They enjoyed the meal and ate just about all of everything we put out.

Then Amadou, somewhat causally, mentioned to Hassanatou their group was going to the local park to see a friend who was playing in a soccer game. He wondered if I could go with them to the game, reminding Hassanatou that Tegan, who she knew, would be coming with the group.

The answer came back, "Yes!" And on the way to the park he bought everyone some ice cream (mine was strawberry).

At the park various people were asking him "who is that girl with your group?"

Amadou was quick to reply, "This is the girl I met today and she is the girl, if we work it out ... who will be my wife!"

Game over. I was informed by Amadou he would take me home. He did and said the goodbyes to my family before he and his friends returned to Austin. It was then my family (Hassanatou, Nasar and the three nieces) asked me,

"Fatima, how would you describe him?"

I slowly answered, "He's okay."

One of my nieces pressed me for more of an opinion, "Do you like him?"

"It's something to think about."

The family said this was all right and noted he is good looking.

* * *

In our next telephone conversation I had with Amadou, he seemed more enthusiastic in his voice expression than previously, and said,

"Oh, Fatima, how are you?"

"I'm fine, was your trip to Austin a safe one?"

"Yes, and thank you for the good food! Fatima ... do you like me?"

"I have to think about it."

"The way I see you now ... I like you! So I will give you three days to think about whether you like me or not."

Chapter 15: The Magnificent Days

Three days came and went. On cue, Amadou called for his clear cut answer. But first we talked of this and that and such. Finally he asked me,

"Fatima, do you like me?"

"Ah, let me think some more about it."

"Please, let me know today. All I need to know now is do you like me."

"Yes, Amadou, ... I like you!"

In a higher pitched voice he exclaimed, "Oh, You like me! Good ... hold the line for one second, are you there?"

"Yes, Amadou, I'm still here."

"Guess what? My dad is now on the line."

The dad quickly said, "Hello there, Fatima."

"Wait dad, this is the girl I'm going to marry!"

Dad responded to this by saying, "Oh, I am glad to meet you"

After a very short pause the mother came on the line, "Hi Fatima, I am excited and happy to talk to you."

"I am happy too."

The mama and I talked (as you might guess) more of this and that and she ended saying "I will give you back to my son," which was followed immediately by Amadou instructing,

"Let me call you right back."

"Amadou, why did you put your parents on the line?"

"You like me, right?"

"Yes, Amadou, that's right."

"I am very happy because that is what I wanted to know. I will hang up now to celebrate my excitement and talk to you later."

*   *   *

Next I called papa in Africa about Amadou

"Oh, Fatima, that's good, where is he from?"

"He is from Guinea, papa."

So, I filled him in on all the details.

"Let me talk to Hassanatou about him."

Hence, I turned the phone over to her and they discussed this in detail.

(Since it is the man's family that formally asks for the hand in marriage we were to await that contact.)

*　　　*　　　*

The next time Amadou and I talked I mentioned one of my cousins was having a graduation party at our house. He said he would come to Dallas and attend the party and he would stay for the entire day. When he arrived he was greeted by my whole extended family. On this visit he consulted with his dad's close elder friend who lived in Dallas.

He told this gentleman he had talked with me; met with me; my family; very much liked me; desired to marry me: and wished to ask for his assistance to ask for my hand.

Expressing himself by asking, "I want to marry her and I need your help, please."

Contemplating this request the elder man said, "Since you have asked my help, this is how we will proceed. I and two other friendly elders of mine will approach Fatima's family and ask for her hand."

Amadou response was, "You know more than I do about these things so whatever you think best is good enough for me"

*　　　*　　　*

Thus one Sunday they came as a group of three to Hassana-tou's house, to discuss at length their proposal and formally ask for my hand in marriage to Amadou!

Chapter 16: Give Me Your Hand, Adoration, And Love

Amadou went to see papa's family and also to formally ask for my hand. A welcome was given and their response was, "We will take this proposal and discuss thoroughly with Hassanatou."

On the day this proposal was put to Hassanatou, Amadou's family had also visited, formally asked for my hand and it was then fully carried out.

The family had gathered for the same reason. "So now" responded Hassanatou, "let me and my husband talk to Fatima and find out exactly what she wants to do!"

Therefore I was approached and informed,

"Fatima, the three gentlemen are asking about a possible marriage and you said that you would get back to them. They are still awaiting and in addition, now Amadou's family has directly and formally asked about this. So now ... Fatima, what do you want? Do you like him well enough to marry him?"

The response I gave to this most important question was a strong, "Yes, I do!"

Hassanatou approached Amadou's family saying, "Fatima's answer is absolutely yes, and tell the family they will always be welcome!"

And so now I have cast my future.

*   *   *

One month later the 'Traditional Wedding' at papa's and mama's home back in Africa was carried out. It was to be one week after this celebration that Ramadan came. This required that I join my husband during this period and cook for him and stay by him. Amadou was to pick me up in Dallas and we would go to Austin during Ramadan.

Since we were to be in Austin everyone in my family was crying because this is where I would live. I asked my ... sister for her forgiveness, if I had ever done anything wrong in the past?

She consoled me by answering, "No, you have never done anything wrong. Go to Austin during Ramadan (which begins at 5 am in the summer morning and ends around 8 pm in the evening) and then we would come back here for the wedding!"

(Technically Hassanatou is my step sister but she has always been so wonderful to me I feel and relate to her as a 'true bonded sister').

*   *   *

I remember during the second week of fasting my husband invited some of the Islamic community to come to his house to 'break the evening fast.'

He said, "Fatima, I'm going to find a lady to assist you in all the cooking."

I said, "No, take me to the supermarket and then I can do all the rest by myself." And I did. Starting on the Saturday morning before the night feast I cooked eight different meals and five varying desserts.

Amadou was working during this time and when he came home around four pm to help me out, he was amazed, surprised and happy that I had done everything for the feast. So when all the people came that Saturday night they exclaimed how much quantity and good food there was, they asked who prepared it?

I modestly said, "I did it myself."

The response from the invited was, "Good job, good food!" Then they all blessed the house.

*   *   *

(Ramadan is to commemorate the revelations of the Qur'an and Fasting is one of the five pillars of the Islamic faith, the other four being: The Profession of Faith; Prayer; Alms; and the Pilgrimage.

As the Arabic lunar calendar is used, it falls 11 short of the solar calendar and so passes through the year in a different fashion, moving through the seasons.

Fasting is required during daylight hours and this includes drinking. Young children, pregnancy and illnesses are not supposed to fast. The period ends when the new crescent moon appears and thus a big holiday is observed: Eid-al-Fitr.)

*   *   *

Three weeks went by and I returned to Dallas to prepare for the 'Wedding'. I especially remember going for the fitting, and you know, this was the happiest day of my life because ... I love weddings!

Hassanatou bought the most important gown of my life for me. The rehearsal was set for Friday and the 'wedding' for Saturday. Hassanatou's friends from all over the US came as did Amadou's numerous friends to attend the Big Day.

It was the best of weddings and the attendees' gifts (along with their pleasant thoughts) filled our entire living room.

Chapter 17: My New Life As A Wife

Wedding over, and my brother Yaya, and sister Aisha, back in Africa are both very happy for me. I had called them and told them I have a very good husband and a good life and live in a good country.

They said to me, "That is fine, you will not have to suffer like us."

I told them, "This life I have now we'll all have together; I will help you and anything I make I will share with you both."

My brother now has nine children and Aisha has five (that's a total of 14, a big bunch of nephews and nieces)!

I instructed them to put the children through school as it is the most important thing to do and I will pay for it. I don't have much but I will do the best I can.

*   *   *

Now back to my marriage. When I came to Austin, Amadou asked me what I wanted to do.

"Someday," I said, "I would like to have a restaurant, but of course we do not have the funds for that so I will start out by braiding hair. Amadou replied that would be okay and added,

"I will continue driving a taxi."

The goal remains the same; to open a food truck or restaurant because I'm a 'good cook.' I have another even grander dream: to buy a house in Africa and bring my brother back to Guinea from the 20 years he had lived in Gambia. Also to buy a second house for my sister and then a third one for me close to them so we could all be together when I visit Africa. Dreams are good to have.

(For about 100,000 dollars in US dollars one can have three houses in Guinea.)

In 2011 I got my citizen's document ('Green Card'). I never thought I would be driving a car, but finally - I did! With the money Amadou and I saved, a car was bought. I learned to drive and got a driver's license. ANYTHING IS POSSIBLE.

*   *   *

I decided to visit my African home-land, so I called Yaya in Gambia and informed him of my coming visit to Guinea. I said,

"Could you come so I can see you there? Then added, "I miss you."

"I miss you too, Fatima, but I can't make it."

"Why not?"

"Because I have no money to travel, I have a lot of children to care for and feed."

I responded, "Can you borrow some money?"

"Okay, I know a guy here that will loan me the money and I will come!"

I suggested Yaya arrive one week before I get there and then and said to him,

"I will give you some money to pay for everything."

My brother became very excited and started to cry. I closed the call saying merely,

"Goodbye, for now."

*   *   *

I chose not to tell my sister that I was coming but make it a surprise to her and also papa Saidou. Mama Ishatou had actually come to Dallas to visit and I told her we would go back together and then bought the plane tickets. It was Friday at the end of the visit when we took off and landed two days later in Africa.

I found papa Saidou was now completely blind. He had been misdiagnosed as having cataracts but in truth had advancing glaucoma and gradually lost his entire sight. He was sitting in his chair when I came into the room and while not being able to see me, I called out, "Papa."

He recognized my voice and asked, "Fatima, is that you?"

"Yes, it is, papa!"

Then he began to cry and I cried with him. He explained all his sight was now all gone, slowly failing after I had gone away. Papa and I talked and talked throughout the afternoon, and included in this discussion was talk about my 'first' husband.

Papa said, "Fatima, I am very sorry about that."

I spoke softly saying, "It's okay, it is in the past, let us forget about that."

I told him I wanted to surprise my sister; and asked if I could use his cell phone. I called Alisha and she first responded by asking,

"How is it you can call me on a Guinea number, Fatima?"

Answering, I said, "Surprise, I'm here at papa's house!"

"Oh, Fatima, you are kidding, right?"

"I am not kidding, sister, here talk to papa."

Now she was very happy and after, talking excitedly to papa, I got the phone back and told her,

"Be ready, I will come and pick you up and we will go to Kiri. Yaya is there and we will stay at grandma Oumou"s house. I haven't told her I am here yet either." (My dad's mom had died a few years before this trip).

Alisha then became over excited but then calmed and reflected,

"Fatima, I don't have any money for a trip."

I responded, "Oh sister, God is Great, don't worry I will take care of you!"

*   *   *

Later on that day, I asked papa what he would want for me to buy for him and being such a nice guy he answered,

"Fatima, I don't need anything, just take something to the village, they are in greater need."

"I know papa, but I want to do something for you. Please let me know what you want."

He paused and then replied, "Well, then buy me some coke and good coffee."

(Coca Cola is fairly expensive in Africa and is a bit of a luxury, as is non-African High Quality European supplied coffee).

"Okay, papa, Mama Ishatou and I will go to the market shortly."

I had four hundred US dollars in my purse and was able to exchange it into four million and eighty Francs. I bought a box-container of Coke, some good coffee, a big box of powdered milk, a can of vegetable oil, tomato paste, spaghetti, large amounts of rice and sugar, and many different vegetables and meats. The home pantry was filled up!

Mama exclaimed, "Papa, Fatima has bought everything!"

Papa's response was, "Fatima, God bless you," and my reply was,

"Well, because of you, I have got to do all this in my life and thank you."

*   *   *

One week later I went to my mother-in-law's house (my husband's mom), which was nearby, and brought this family a lot of food also. I followed up by visiting my sister's house, which was also nearby, and we visited with joy.

"Alisha," I said, "let us go to the market, I want to buy some food and also some clothes for you and the children (in addition I purchased some food and clothes for both of my stepmothers in Kiri). Then I left for our old village.

*   *   *

When I had arrived in the still small village of Kiri, my brother, sister and I went house-to-house giving a little money to the people. They often would run out of funds before the next weekly visit to the market because their husbands did not have enough money to tide them over. At that time my blind grandma, Oumou, was still alive so after we left Alisha's house and finished our walk around the village my sister, brother and I went to visit grandma; she did not know any of us were coming!

My uncle, Sorh was there with her also. Entering the house Omou was sitting in a chair and without saying anything the three sat down around her. My brother had not seen her in 15 years and neither I or my sister had seen her for a long time. Yaya began by slowly rubbing her legs.

"Oh!" she said, "I smell something, Yaya can that be you?"

"Yes, grandma, it is me!"

Omou began crying and I greeted her, "Hello grandma."

She had a questioning look on her face and asked, "Alisa, is that you?"

I responded, "It is Fatima!"

"Oh! Fatima - that is you!"

"Yes, grandma."

She started shaking and crying. I asked her,

"Don't cry, my sister Alisha is also here!"

Along with being blind grandma was seen not to be in good health yet she responded,

"I need to get up today with all of you here."

So, then everybody started hugging everyone else.

Grandma arose and happily exclaimed, "Let's find something we can all eat."

We found there were peanuts, dried fish, and rice stored up in the attic eaves and believe it or not she climbed up a ladder by herself, and retrieved the food.

Uncle Sorh, was amazed at grandma's determined skill to be able to do this at her age. He told us the last time she was able to do this was the year before and she had not tried since. Yet today while we were all there she did it!

Everyone helped out; we got the fire going; cooked and prepared the food; set everything in order: and sat down to a wonderful dinner. During dinner, grandma was pleased to tell me, over and over, that she had received all my gifts from America I had sent her, by way of sister Alisha.

I told her she was very deserving and that she was most welcome and that I thought of her always.

*   *   *

In my village of Kiri the people are suffering with a particular problem; the obtaining of a supply of fresh, close at hand, drinkable water. My dream is to help them have potable water in this village so they do not have to walk over one hour to the river and back to get it. They have the need to carry it in containers on their heads every day! Also the children, to be in school, have to journey two miles out and back to the teaching site, often arriving at home in the dark.

Seeing this method of water supply caused me to remember the last time I was in Kiri and we needed the daily water. My sister, Alisha, decided we would make the trip to the river. It had been hot and dry for a number of days and the drought was as hard on the animals, as it was on the villagers. Not long after we set out we met up with a lot of thirsty cows, who well knew the way to the river, and their large number of cows which frightened me a little. We got to the river, collected the water and were blessed on our one hour return to be again accompanied by these bovine animals. I cannot forget that this is an exercise the village women are called on to do - every day.

If I get the opportunity in the future I would desire to build a school site for the children in Kiri. I know I can do this because God will help me. My vision is also to develop a local 'firm' for the ladies of the village in which they will be able to make produce and then sell it in the market, bettering their family's daily lives.

I love helping people and to see their smiles and lessened sufferings. I believe everything happens for a reason and people change as they learn and observe the better things in life.

When something goes wrong and falls apart we need to believe good things may well be coming 'to fall together.'

So, learn to appreciate where you come from, what you can achieve and be happy with your life!

*   *   *

In Africa mama and papa taught me how to live, to apply myself and to handle many activities. Although they'd not send me to school, I was to learn many experiences of life; domestic responsibilities; self discipline; how to evaluate people; importance of learning skills; development of my own ideas: and what is good and right.

      This is the way I live today in America. Whenever hired in a position I apply to the work and do my best for those whom I am in contact with, to make them happy in me. Presently my income is not a lot but I can support Alisha's children's study in school and also Yaya's. Much to my delight they are all doing well in their studies and learning.

      All these wondrous things have become possible because of mama and papa and I thank them a million times!

      In addition I deeply thank Hassanatou for putting me in ESL as I have learned so much, including English speaking, spelling and writing. She is my great joy!

Chapter 18: A Wonderful Husband And A Bit Of My Philosophy

When I believe some action and thought will be good for me, my approach is to give my prayers requesting it, and little by little, I know they will be answered; I don't give up.

I am going to be a good wife and also appreciate everything that has come into my life, especially my husband, Amadou; he is an excellent man. When we were first married I became aware he did not care for doing the laundry very much, that, and in addition to cleaning the house. When I applied a little pressure for him to do the wash he would do something like putting too much soap with clothes hoping he wouldn't be asked to do the task again. I realized I would have to give in and do it all by myself yet with my working also, coming home from work was really too much of a chore for me alone.

So, I thought, perhaps I could find some inducement to get him to help with cleaning and washing by making his favorite dishes and being the best of all housewives. Also I noticed he loves my smiles whenever he opens the front door coming in from work. This, I think, is good psychology! Now I get all the help I need.

Whatever is good in life for you should be good for others. If someone treats you with disrespect, return pleasantness of a kind you would like yourself and then they will respond in kind - most of the time.

                    *   *   *

One time I must admit this did not work out satisfactory. I
was working for an emergency room lady doctor, whose husband was also a doctor, and they lived in a large, beautiful
house. They had two children, whom I liked very much and
the three of us played around a lot which was an enjoyment
of this position.

   The wife quite easily got upset and directed her dis-
comfort toward me, often yelling and even screaming, when
there was no cause for it. It made me cry sometimes because
I did not want to leave this job. The two children noticed
their mother's unfair attitude toward me, but they liked me.

   One night, quite late, the lady called me at home and
asked me to come to her house early to watch the children as
she had to go into work sooner than usual. I had actually
come a bit earlier than she even requested. As I opened the
front door she pointedly spoke to her children in a voice I
could not hear,

      "What is this idiot girl doing here so early?"

   I said my usual greeting to her,

      "Good morning."

   She turned with a bright smile and tone of voice,

      "Oh, good morning to you, it is good you came early."

Later on I learned from the older of the two children that their mom had called me an idiot and I asked,

"Do you children think I am an idiot?"

They both said,

"Oh no, we love you and you are a smart person."

I then decided not to respond unless this disrespect occurred again. In fact if it persisted after two future occasions I would leave this job even though I needed it!

On the third occurrence she really laid into me by screaming and yelling for no apparent reason and I knew I must talk to her about this problem. I told her,

"Don't yell at me, please, if I do something wrong just talk to me and tell me why you are so upset. If you do this disrespect once again I will need to leave."

She made no apology or an adequate response. That evening I called my boss and discussed the entire problem with her. She understood and said,

"Do not worry, I will talk to her and it won't happen again."

The following day the lady presented me with an expensive, but now too small size dress of hers and apologized for her behavior to me. I accepted the apology. Situation solved? No, not for very long.

Two weeks later the lady went on a vacation, leaving me with the children and their grandmother. Her first day back she walked in while the grandma was feeding the three year old at the kitchen table. When the child saw the mother she got excited and she knocked the dish off on the floor (faced down of course).

The mom lost it. She started screaming at me asking,

"Why did the dish fall, what's going on?" Then followed a long list of unnecessary complaints, mainly directed at me, supported by aggressive stares and frowns.

I said nothing as the younger child came over to me and gave me a hug saying she was sorry for all this. I cleaned up the floor knowing I would no longer put up with this abuse. That night I contacted the boss and told her I would give two weeks notice for a replacement to come, for the children's sake. The boss agreed and said she would inform the lady.

The next day, as work started, the emergency room doctor began by begging me again not to leave. During this tenseness she offered to give money 'on the side' to remain, saying,

Don't tell your boss about this additional money, okay?"

I responded, "No, it's not okay."

"Oh, go ahead and take it!"

"I must tell the boss if I receive extra money."

This seemed to make no difference one way or another.

"Are you really going to leave?"

"Yes, I am."

Later in the day the boss called me and informed me the doctor was willing to give me a raise.

My answer to my boss was, I told her no,

"Even though I have no other job lined up, I am leaving my employment here!"

*   *   *

The remaining two weeks were filled with her excuses and apologies and a promise of a raise and even how the entire family appreciated me.

My only remarks were,

"I'm done, it is okay, and good luck to you all. That last day delivered the joy of leaving, in spite of now having no job lined up.

The last insult to me came from her when she instructed my boss not to recommend me to any of her friends for a job. It all worked out, as two week later, the boss found me another job with better paid and in a very good family for the next four years and it has been a joy.

*   *   *

My husband and I have been married for 13 years. He has one fine son, Ismail, who is now 14 years old, attending high school, and is a very good student. We get along great together. Amadou and I tried for another child but sadly it was not to come. Yet it is better to be happy with what you have than be discouraged with what you don't. He is nice to me so I am blessed.

On rare occasions we do, I confess, argue a little, but never seriously - he is a good man, the very best. We also have our little strengths and weaknesses. For instance he is not totally good at going to the market, like, ask him to buy one orange and you may get ten. We both enjoy home cooked food and are interested in having a food truck or small restaurant in time.

What really matters ... we both love one another!

Chapter 19: And For The Future... It Holds Today's Dreams

Amadou and I plan to save our money and begin business with a food truck and when the time is right open an African Food restaurant.

The ethnic foods will be from Gambia, Senegal and the Ivory Coast areas. I choose these foods because I have had a long experience in their cooking and most importantly, I have been told by many, I am a very good chef.

So, as you know, in America if you apply yourselves to a dream it will come true. This I truly believe.

I continue to work at developing into a good business woman, eventually acquiring a house of our own and living in joyfulness with my husband and our many close friends.

ADDITIONAL LAST WORDS

I want to thank Allah for making me happy all the time. And secondly, I wish to thank the most important people in my life.

First, is to be papa Sadou and mama Ishatou for teaching me to be a good person and also in their care of me.

My sister Hassanatou, comes next, for her trust in me and bringing me to the USA. It is because of her I can spell and even write a book. I say to her, thank you, I will always keep you in my heart.

I thank my husband Amadou, for always being there for me; I love you.

The friendship of Alloua has been most important to me as has my American niece, Rougi with her thoughtfulness.

Also I want to express my feelings for the help and kindness of Dr. Mike and his wife Beverly who I have worked for over the last four years.

And lastly, I must thank my two best friends, Kidjida and Sally, for always being supportive and kind to me.

... And think not you can direct the course of love,

for love, if it finds you worthy, directs your
course

Kahlil Gibran

Made in the USA
Columbia, SC
11 July 2021